Deleted

W9-ACT-224

EXCEPTIONAL
ASIANS

MAYA LIN

Artist and
Architect

Cecelia H. Brannon

Enslow Publishing
101 W. 23rd Street
Suite 240
New York, NY 10011
USA

enslow.com

Words to Know

architect—A person who designs buildings.

autobiography—A book an author writes about herself.

ceramicist—An artist who works with ceramics, a material made from clay.

committee—A group that is formed to get something done.

contemplation—A time to think deeply about something serious.

etched—Carved on a hard surface such as wood or stone.

granite—A hard, crystal-like rock made from hardened lava that is shiny when polished.

immigrant—A person who moves to another country.

memorial—A structure designed to remind people of a particular person or event.

Contents

R0452299463

Maya Lin

CHAPTER 1

A Young Artist

Maya Lin is a world-famous **architect** and sculptor. She is considered a national treasure in the United States. Her sculptures and buildings can be found all across the country, and even as far away as New Zealand.

Maya Lin was born on October 5, 1959, in Athens, Ohio. Her parents were Chinese **immigrants**. Maya came from a long line of artists. Her father, Henry Huan Lin, was a **ceramicist** and dean of the College of Fine Arts at the University of Ohio. Her mother, Julia Chang Lin, was a poet and a literature professor at the same school. Maya's great-aunt, Lin Huiyin, was the first female architect in China. Maya has an older brother, Tan, who became a poet like their mother.

A Quiet Childhood

Growing up, Maya admits she was a bit of a nerd. She didn't have many friends, and she enjoyed reading and math. She also liked spending time outdoors, hiking and bird watching. She studied a lot, even taking classes at the University of Ohio when she was in high school. She built models of

Maya Says:

"Math. It's a puzzle to me. I love figuring out puzzles."

High School, Athens, Ohio

Maya attended this high school in Athens, Ohio, while also taking college classes.

towns she hoped to someday build, cast bronze sculptures in the university's metal workshop, and created ceramics in her father's studio.

Despite her Chinese roots, Maya did not consider herself Chinese. In fact, she didn't even realize she wasn't white until she went to college and experienced a bit of racism.

Maya attended Yale University, studying art and architecture. It was here that Maya's life would change forever.

CHAPTER 2

Vietnam Veterans Memorial

In 1959, the United States began to send soldiers to South Vietnam to help the people there defend themselves against North Vietnam. For sixteen years, thousands of American men and women fought and gave their lives to protect the freedom of these people on the other side of the world.

A National Contest

In 1980, a contest was held to find a design for a **memorial** in Washington, DC, to honor the fallen soldiers from the Vietnam War. There were four requirements: the memorial must make no political statement on the war itself, it must fit in with the rest of the National Mall, it had to be a place of **contemplation** and prayer, and it must list the names of the dead and missing soldiers from Vietnam. Only Americans could apply.

In 1981, one of Maya's professors asked her class to design something based on these requirements. She did this and sent it to the **committee**, in hopes of being chosen. Her professor gave her a B+.

The National Mall stretches from the US Capitol to the Washington Monument.

All eight judges selected Maya's design. It beat out 1,441 other entries. She was just twenty-one and had not even graduated from college yet.

When the winning designer was announced, many people were upset. Not only was Maya very young, but she was also a Chinese American

Young Maya with her design and Jan Scruggs, founder of the Vietnam Veterans Memorial Fund.

woman. During the Vietnam War, China had supported North Vietnam. Others said the design was too modern and wouldn't fit in with the other monuments.

But Maya didn't back down. She believed in her design, and that Americans needed a place to heal from the war. It was finally decided that two other sculptures would be put up along with the memorial wall. On March 26, 1982, construction began. It was completed in October of that year. On Veteran's Day (November 11) 1982, the wall was opened to the public.

The Memorial Wall

The Vietnam Veterans Memorial Wall is made of polished, black **granite**. The wall is shaped like a wide V, with the Lincoln Memorial at one end and the Washington Monument at the other. Maya said

Maya Says:

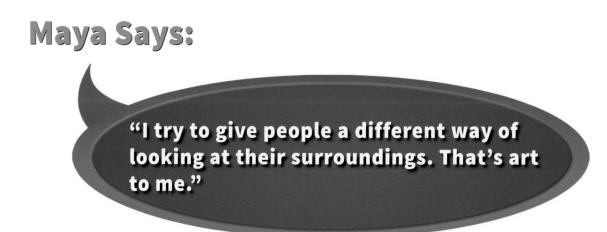

"I try to give people a different way of looking at their surroundings. That's art to me."

she shaped it this way so that it would represent the wound that war had created in Americans.

Etched into the wall are the names of the 58,286 soldiers who either died in Vietnam or are considered missing in action. There is no mention of the soldiers' rank, gender, race, or religion on the wall, showing that each loss was equal to others.

Beside each name is a symbol. The diamond symbol notes that the solider is declared dead. The cross shape represents soldiers that are missing. Every May, sculptors add to the wall, replacing

The names on the Vietnam Veterans Memorial are arranged by the date of death of each soldier.

As many as ten thousand people visit the wall every day. It is the most visited place in Washington, DC.

crosses with diamonds as the bodies of American soldiers are found in Vietnam. There is a third symbol, a star surrounding the cross, to represent soldiers that have been found. That symbol has never been used.

CHAPTER 3
Not Just a Memorial Artist

Although Maya may be best known for her design of the Vietnam Veterans Memorial, it is far from her only work.

In 1989, Maya designed the Civil Rights Memorial in Montgomery, Alabama. The memorial is a fountain with the names of forty-one people who lost their lives in the civil rights movement between 1954 and 1968. The final name on the wall is that of civil rights leader Dr. Martin Luther King Jr. A line from his "I Have a Dream" speech inspired the work: "We will not be satisfied until justice rolls down like water and

Maya stands near the Civil Rights Memorial in Montgomery, Alabama.

righteousness like a mighty stream." Maya hoped the water would soothe people who were still angry about injustices in America during that time.

Over the next few years, Maya created many sculptures that were seen by many all over the United States, including *Eclipsed Time* in New York

City, *Women's Table* at Yale, and *Groundswell* in Columbus, Ohio. Each piece fits the area where it was made and has special meaning to Maya.

More Than Sculptures and Memorials

In 1992, Maya designed her first building, the Museum for African Art in New York City. This was something she truly enjoyed. In 1999, she designed another building, the Langston Hughes Library in Clinton, Tennessee. She went on to create the Riggio-Lynch Chapel, also in Clinton, Tennessee, and the Arts Plaza at Claire Trevor School of the Arts in Irvine, California.

Maya Says:

"The process I go through in art and architecture, I actually want it to be almost childlike."

Maya is also a landscape architect, meaning the she creates sculptures outdoors from materials such as plants and rocks. Outdoor pieces such as *Wave Field* in Ann Arbor, Michigan, *Input* in Athens, Ohio, and *A Fold in the Field* in Kaipara Harbour, New Zealand, show Maya's love of nature.

Maya stands with her *Bodies of Water* series.

18

CHAPTER 4

Maya Today

Maya Lin married photographer David Wolf in 1996. They have two daughters, India and Rachel. The same year she married, Maya began designing and rebuilding an apartment in Manhattan, a labor of love for her family.

In 2000, Maya released her **autobiography**, *Boundaries*, in which she discusses her life, her views of the world, and how she creates her art.

Awarded Artist

In 2003, Maya served on the selection jury of the World Trade Center Memorial, helping to create the memorial in New York City for the Americans who lost their lives during the terrorist attacks of September 11, 2001. Two years later, she was elected into the National Women's Hall of Fame. In 2009, President Barack Obama awarded her the National Medal of Arts.

Still at Work

Maya still finds time to create her art. In 2009, she began a project called *What Is Missing?* This project, which has parts in various locations, is designed to make people aware of the loss of natural habitats for wildlife. She hopes, through art, to create a better planet for us all to share.

In 2015, Maya released *Topologies*, a book of photographs of her work. She has also agreed to

design a new home for the Museum of Chinese in America, a project that speaks to her. She wants her daughters, as well as all Asian American children, to know their culture and be proud of it.

Over her thirty-three-year career, Maya Lin has created beautiful art that makes people think. She inspires artists of all ages and backgrounds and has made an important place for herself in United States culture and history.

Maya receives the National Medal of Arts from President Obama.

Timeline

1959—Maya Lin is born in Athens, Ohio.

1979—Attends Yale University.

1981—Wins competition to design the Vietnam Veterans Memorial in Washington, DC. Receives bachelor's degree from Yale.

1982—Vietnam Veterans Memorial is built.

1986—Receives master's degree in architecture from Yale.

1989—Designs the Civil Rights Memorial in Montgomery, Alabama.

1992—Designs the Museum of African Art in New York City.

1996—Marries David Wolf.

1999—Designs Langston Hughes Library in Clinton, Tennessee.

2000—Writes autobiography *Boundaries*.

2003—Serves on selection jury for the design of the World Trade Center Memorial.

2005—Elected into American Academy of Arts and Letters and the National Women's Hall of Fame.

2009—Awarded the National Medal of Arts by President Obama.

2015—Asked to design the new library at Smith College in Northampton, Massachusetts. Releases *Topologies.*

Learn More

Books

Alexander, Heather, and Meredith Hamilton. *Child's Introduction to Art: The World's Greatest Paintings and Sculptures*. New York: Black Dog and Levinthal, 2014.

Finger, Brad. *13 American Artists All Kids Should Know*. New York: Random House, 2010.

Kohl, MaryAnn F., and Kim Solga. *Great American Artists for Kids: Hands-On Art Experiences in the Styles of Great American Masters*. New York: Bright Ring Publishing, 2008.

Lin, Maya. *Topologies*. New York: Rizzoli, 2015.

Websites

www.mayalin.com
Maya Lin's official website, where you can see examples of her work.

www.whatismissing.net
The official website of Maya Lin's project *What Is Missing?*

www.nps.gov/vive/index.htm
The official website of the Vietnam Veterans Memorial Wall, run by the National Park Service.

Index

Published in 2017 by Enslow Publishing, LLC.
101 W. 23rd Street, Suite 240, New York, NY 10011

Copyright © 2017 by Enslow Publishing, LLC.
All rights reserved.

No part of this book may be reproduced by any means without the written permission of the publisher.

Library of Congress Cataloging-in-Publication Data
Names: Brannon, Cecelia H., author.
Title: Maya Lin : Artist and Architect / Cecelia H. Brannon.
Description: New York : Enslow Publishing, [2017] | Series: Exceptional Asians | Includes bibliographical references and index.
Identifiers: LCCN 2015044484| ISBN 9780766078383 (library bound) | ISBN 9780766078444 (pbk.) | ISBN 9780766078048 (6-pack)
Subjects: LCSH: Lin, Maya Ying. | Asian American artists--Biography--Juvenile literature. | Asian American architects--Biography--Juvenile literature.
Classification: LCC N6537.L54 B73 2016 | DDC 720.92--dc23
LC record available at http://lccn.loc.gov/2015044484

Printed in Malaysia

To Our Readers: We have done our best to make sure all website addresses in this book were active and appropriate when we went to press. However, the author and the publisher have no control over and assume no liability for the material available on those websites or on any websites they may link to. Any comments or suggestions can be sent by e-mail to customerservice@enslow.com.

Photo Credits: Throughout book, ©Toria/Shutterstock.com (blue background); cover, p. 1 Brian Ach/Getty Images Entertainment/Getty Images; p. 4 Brad Barket/Getty Images; p 7. MUL Collection/Alamy Stock Photo; p. 9 Carol M. Highsmith/Buyenlarge/Getty Images; p. 10 James M. Thresher/The Washington Post via Getty Images; p. 13 Anh Nguyen/Moment Editorial/Getty Images, Win McNamee/Getty Images (inset); p. 14 Bill O'Leary/The Washington Post via Getty Images; p. 16 Thomas S. England/The LIFE Images Collection/Getty Images; p. 18 Lois Raimondo/The Washington Post/Getty Images; p. 21 MIKE THEILER/UPI/Newscom.